WHAT IS A

SCHIZOPHRENIC

SUPPOSED

TO LOOK LIKE?

Fourth Edition

Lori Rochat

What Is A Schizophrenic Supposed To Look Like?
Fourth Edition

Lori Rochat, Author

Jill M. Riga, Contributing Editor

Michael T. Petro, Jr., General Editor
Published by Petro Publications
PetroPublications.com

Front Cover Photo:
Schizophrenia word written on medical blue folder
ID 79491894 © Andrianocz / *Dreamstime.com*

ISBN-13: 978-1-7337041-0-6

Dedication

I dedicate this book to my mother for helping me with the topic selections for this book. In addition, I am eternally grateful to her for being there for me throughout life's struggles, and for guiding me on my path toward wellness. My Aunt Carol must also receive recognition for referring me to Dr. Herbert Meltzer's study, which dramatically improved my life. Also, I would like to thank Matt Sucre from the Cleveland Public Library for helping me to get started with this project and for referring me to Jill M. Riga, a contributing editor to this book. Lastly, I wish to thank Michael T. Petro, Jr., an author, editor, and publisher at Petro Publications. He served as the general editor and helped me make this book become a reality.

Table Of Contents

Introduction

I would like the reader to understand my motivation for writing this book. The diagnosis of schizophrenia can be as disturbing as the symptoms one experiences with this form of illness. I wrote this book because every life experience I have had relates to my mental illness in some way, and I wish to share those experiences with others. I love helping people and have compassion for the mentally ill. I understand the challenges they face and have a deep desire to help them deal with those challenges as effectively as possible.

The word schizophrenia is scary to many people and it conjures up stereotypic images of a gloomy or dangerous individual. I titled my book, *What is a Schizophrenic Supposed to Look Like?* to shine a little light on the fact that the general public often comes into contact with people living with schizophrenia in their daily lives — but they are unable to distinguish them from so-called "normal" people within the general population! They are unable to spot them in a crowd!

So, to help end the widespread misunderstanding people have about schizophrenia and to stop the stigma that follows, I would like readers to ask themselves, "What is a schizophrenic supposed to look like?" I want them to know that when they describe a schizophrenic in stereotypic terms, they are usually wrong because it is not a "look!"

What Is A Schizophrenic Supposed To Look Like?

There is a website called *Schizophrenia.com* where people with schizophrenia can communicate with others who have the same illness. Sometimes people say to me when I am stabilized on my medication, "You don't look schizophrenic." So my question to the people on this website was, "What is a schizophrenic supposed to look like?" I received some interesting responses.

Most all who responded admitted that they didn't know what a schizophrenic is supposed to look like although they had schizophrenia themselves. One respondent said that an individual with schizophrenia was someone who dressed in old clothing and didn't wash too often. Another stated that he looked normal but he dressed in black "like a Sith," which as Star Wars fans know is an alien race with a terrifying appearance and devoted to "the Dark Side." One reported that he "looks okay" except for some involuntary jaw movements and as one would expect, he found these movements to be "annoying." Lastly, an individual said that he can "blend in well" with others on the job or at a restaurant. He also stated that he "fits in so well" most anywhere that he wonders if "maybe the guy sitting next to me in the restaurant is a schizophrenic blending in too!"

At this point, I would like to state that people with physical disabilities, such as those in wheelchairs, cannot hide their disabilities. But because mental illness is an internal disability, it can be hidden from the public. Yet people with schizophrenia who are not stabilized on medication do expose their mental disability when they talk to themselves or say things that do not make sense.

It appears that when people with schizophrenia are asked, "What is a schizophrenic supposed to look like?" the answer is unclear, based on responses provided at *Schizophrenia.com*.

What Is A High-Functioning Schizophrenic?

The second question I asked people who subscribed to the website *Schizophrenia.com* was as follows: "What is a high-functioning schizophrenic?" Once again, I received some very interesting responses.

One respondent said, "I consider myself a high-functioning schizophrenic. I own a home, own a car, have been married, and have raised a child. I rely on medicine to get through the day, but I am not in intensive therapy. I make my own decisions and can feed, dress, and entertain myself."

After trying three different medications one female respondent said, "I'm high-functioning." She added, "Life is normal. I have friends, work, have a degree and I'm thinking of going to grad school." She says the guys she dates sometimes "crack crazy people jokes" and they "have no clue" she has schizophrenia. When not taking her medication she suffers from delusions and she hears voices. When taking medications that didn't work, she said that "life really sucked!" However, now that she has found a medication that works, "Life is just fine," as long as she takes her medication.

Some stated that they may be high-functioning sometimes but not at all times because they have good days and bad days.

My Life Before Schizophrenia

My childhood was basically normal except for perhaps a few unusual circumstances. Unfortunately, my father died when I was only eight years old. My mother, a secretary at that time, faced the task of raising me and my brother by herself. Her company moved a lot, and as a consequence, so did we!

During high school summer break I got a job at Mr. Chicken at the age of 16. I loved that job! After graduating from high school I stayed at my grandmother's house and got a job at a hotel. During this time period I had no idea what I wanted to do with my life even though I studied cosmetology in high school. While staying with my grandmother she began to notice unusual behavior on my part. For example, I would stay awake all night listening to music and I could not sleep even one hour due to hearing relentless voices. I thought the music would drown out the voices, but it did not. My grandmother called my mom to come get me and take me home because of my bizarre behavior. This signified the beginning of my struggle with mental illness, and as one would expect, this led to my hospitalization.

Schizophrenia: Are You One In One Hundred?

Did you know that one in one hundred people have schizophrenia? Schizophrenia is a thought disorder characterized by delusions, hallucinations, paranoia, and social isolation. Schizophrenia can be controlled with medication, but there is no known cure at this time. Symptoms of schizophrenia tend to appear during the teenage years and sometimes well into the late 30's. I personally suffer from paranoid schizophrenia.

Now I am going to tell you the story of how I found out I had schizophrenia. No one in my family and none of my friends ever had or understood schizophrenia. It started when I was 17 years old. I was getting panic attacks, and my grades in high school started to deteriorate. I became depressed and suicidal. After high school, I started experiencing paranoia and delusional thoughts. For example, I thought my neighbors were spying on me, my phone was bugged, and that there were cameras in the house. I thought my mother was putting poison in my food, people could read my mind, and I thought the TV and newspapers were about me.

In addition, I was laughing at things that were not funny. I was hearing voices telling me I was psychic, and I was not sleeping well. My mother thought I was on street drugs, so she said she wanted to take me to the hospital for drug testing. I told her I was not taking any street drugs, but she did not believe me so she took me to the hospital anyway. They drug-tested me and discovered I had no drugs in my system. I was mad at my mom for taking me there and I did not want to stay. I kicked my mom's chair and told her she was crazy for taking me there.

Should you need help in getting a person to the hospital when they do not want to cooperate, this is the point at which you would call the police and ask for a CIT-trained police officer (Crisis Intervention Team) to assist you.

Upon arrival to the hospital I learned about involuntary admission, or the placement of a person under psychiatric care without their consent. If mentally ill people are out of control, aggressive, or at serious risk of harming themselves or others, they can be involuntarily admitted to a hospital to receive treatment under an Emergency Certificate.

Once admitted, I tried to get off the psychiatric ward when someone opened the door. I simply snuck out. I started to run and made a phone call to a friend, telling her to come get me, but two police officers found me and brought me back to the psychiatric ward. The hospital staff told my mom to leave and they locked me up in a room with only a bed. My first thought was, "How can I escape?" There was a window that I thought I could jump out of, but there was no way to open it and it was far too high to reach. When the hospital staff opened my door, I tried to push them away and escape, but I did not succeed.

Eventually the hospital staff opened my door and said, "If you remain calm, we will let you out of your room." I said, "Okay," because I felt like I was in jail. I wandered around and asked a male patient, "What are you in here for?" He said, "Schizophrenia!" I was so afraid of him that I would not go near him. Later, I was told that I had schizophrenia, and all I remember is the hospital staff telling me I needed to take a medication called Haldol.

Finally, after three long months, they released me. One year after being discharged from this Cleveland-area hospital, I joined Dr. Herbert Meltzer's study to test a new medication called Clozapine (Clozaril) for schizophrenia. This was an outpatient program that lasted two years. While in this outpatient program, I learned that research trials are a great way to test a variety of new medications to see which ones could work best for you when you have not found a medication to stabilize you.

When the two-year study was over, they took me off Clozapine (Clozaril) to try other medications to see what would happen. I wound up in the hospital again for another three months. This time it was not as scary because I had become an experienced hospital inpatient. Again, I felt like I was in prison. I remember I wanted to get out of there so badly I started screaming, "Let me out of here!" They moved me to a room with just a mattress and padded walls. I remember crying and crying. When I calmed down, they let me back onto the general ward.

A psychiatric ward can be scary at times because some of the other patients can be very intimidating. For example, one female patient wanted to pick a fight with me, and a male patient tried to rape me. The hospital staff moved him to another floor. After three long months, they put me back on Clozapine (Clozaril) and I was released once again. Without medication my quality of life would be terrible.

Getting Your Medical Records

Everyone is entitled to have access to their medical records. I have copies of mine. Copies can cost as much as one dollar per page, but they are worth every penny.

First of all, you have to sign a release of information to get your medical records. Sometimes they charge you if you go over the limit of free copies. The reason you have to sign a release of information form is because no one can get your records without your permission. If anyone releases your medical records without your consent, it breaks the HIPPA Privacy Rule. (Google "HIPPA" if you have to file a complaint.) If you want to change something in your medical records, you have a right to amend them if you feel your health information is incorrect or incomplete. Your request for an amendment must be in writing, signed, and dated, and specify the record or records you wish to amend.

Also, the most important thing to know about getting medical records when you have a mental illness is that you can get everything except the physician's notes. Physician's notes are private notes and you need permission from your psychiatrist to gain access to them. When I inquired about this restriction, I was told by a medical records office worker that a patient killed herself after reading the notes taken by her psychiatrist. So, before they can be released, the attending psychiatrist must first determine if the patient can handle the material in the physician's notes.

My Medical Records

My medical records from my hospitalization in 1990 fill a huge notebook. I want to share with the reader a few paragraphs from my medical records.

CHIEF COMPLAINT AND HISTORY OF PRESENT ILLNESS:

The patient is a 20-year-old single white female who came into the E.R. several nights prior to admission in an agitated state. She was preoccupied with delusions that she had about her neighbor. She gave a history of having been fairly depressed with high anxiety for at least the past three years, and she had experienced frequent panic attacks and anxiety to the extent that she had not been able to hold down jobs. She stated that her spirits had been low fairly continually during the past three years and that she had had frequent suicidal thoughts which she had never acted upon. She had an interest in her neighbor, Bob, throughout much of this time, but apparently became delusional about him about nine months prior to admission when she apparently became quite certainly convinced that this married neighbor was in love with her, and that he was sending signals to her by the way that he would park his car or the way that he would close his curtains in his house. Her delusions began to extend to the point where she felt some kind of merger between her family and his family was evident. Her agitation surrounding these delusions had been steadily increasing and in the week prior to admission, she had stopped eating, and she was sleeping very little. She also began to fear that her own house had been bugged. Her mother brought her to the hospital on 9/19 and she was admitted on an Emergency Certificate. She began expressing paranoid thoughts about Dr. Smith, thinking the medication that she had been given had something "funny" in it.

MENTAL STATUS EXAMINATION:

In the E.R., the patient was alert and talked incessantly, often twisting her sunglasses. Her mood was depressed with positive suicidal ideations. She had inappropriate affect with frequent inappropriate smiling. Her speech was incessant and slightly pressured. Her thoughts were tangential. She had delusions regarding her next-door neighbor, and his involvement in her life. She had vague suicidal ideations, but no intent. She had no homicidal ideations. There was no evidence of hallucinations. On cognitive exam, she was oriented to person, place, and situation, but she was two days off in time. She had decreased attention span. Her short-term memory appeared to be intact, but her long-term memory was questionable.

HOSPITAL COURSE:

At the time of admission, the patient was very delusional, paranoid, and agitated. It was necessary to place her in lock and seclusion. On hospital day one, she was given a total of 35 mg of

Haldol in divided doses, and she was given Moban 10 mg bid. She responded to this medication, and she had some softening of her delusions overnight. She tolerated the medication well except for some orthostatic hypotension. Because of her continual agitation on hospital day two, Ativan 2 mg bid was added. By the third day of hospitalization, she was able to be on the ward. She still had delusions, but she was not planning her life around them. The Haldol was decreased to 5 mg bid, and the Ativan was decreased to 1 mg bid. She remained on this with gradual improvement for several days. She continued to have problems with orthostatic hypotension and with tiredness. On 9/25/90, her Ativan was increased to 4 mg daily in divided doses and her Haldol was increased to 7 mg bid. At this time, by the following day, she had very little evidence of active psychosis. She obviously still had difficulty holding to her thoughts, but she realized that her thoughts regarding her next-door neighbor were delusional. She desired discharge, and this appeared to be a possibility.

What It's Like To Have Schizophrenia

Having schizophrenia is not fun. For the rest of my life, I have to go every month to get my blood drawn. If my white blood cell count is low (which is called agranulocytosis), I must have it drawn once each week or every two weeks. If my white blood cell count is too low, I can't get my prescription. I have tried other medications, but Clozapine (Clozaril) is the only medication that works for me. I never want to be hospitalized again, so I must always take my medication.

I see a psychiatrist once a month. I need twelve hours of sleep because the medication is very sedating. The medication makes me gain weight, so I have to exercise and watch what I eat. Those are the physical problems I experience with schizophrenia. The psychological and social problems center around the fact that some people are uncomfortable around me when I tell them I have schizophrenia, or they crack "crazy people" jokes!

Understanding Voices

Every person I know with schizophrenia has heard voices, and I'm not talking about voices originating from a person sitting next to you, or voices conveyed over the telephone or some other communication device. I'm talking about voices that originate from a source that can only be heard by the individual with schizophrenia. I'm talking about auditory hallucinations, which are voices that originate within the psyche of the individual.

The voices can tell the individual to believe that which is truly unbelievable, or to believe that which is not true. Also, the voices can instruct the individual to do things that may be irrational, or even dangerous. For example, I remember my mother walking upstairs to check on me one night, and the voices told me that she had a knife and was coming to kill me. Of course, that was not true, but I was naturally very frightened and could have mistakenly taken defensive action against her. So, even very trustworthy family members can be falsely described as untrustworthy or threatening by hallucinatory, accusatory voices.

Sometimes a person with schizophrenia may stay awake all night — and every night — for an extended period of time because they cannot turn off the internal voices, like the time I was at my grandmother's.

Strangely enough, while the voices may originate from within the psyche of the individual, a person with schizophrenia may believe some voices originate from a television set or even a newspaper. Clearly, auditory hallucinations can be very disturbing and confusing because the individual cannot distinguish between what is real and what is not real. When you see people talking to themselves, you know they are responding to voices that no one else can hear. This is a classic symptom of schizophrenia!

Schizophrenia And Religious Delusions

Oftentimes schizophrenia can cause religious delusions. When I was cleaning a drawer one day, I found something I wrote on a piece of paper. It mentioned weird religious experiences. Here is what I wrote:

Felt like the devil was going to kill me. I panicked and read the Bible. Felt like Jesus' spirit was inside my mind. Felt like Jesus was giving psychic messages. I thought my black cat was the devil and wanted to squirt her with water thinking it was holy water.

When hospitalized I thought I was Jesus. I was afraid of evil spirits and had to sleep with the light on. In spite of these delusions, I am religious.

Panic Attacks And Anxiety

Not only do I deal with schizophrenia, but I also suffer from panic attacks and anxiety. Just recently I went to the bank to cash a check, and I was standing in line and all of a sudden I got a hot flash and felt dizzy. I tried to grab on to the pole that was next to me. And I told the woman behind me that I was having an anxiety attack. Then one of the bankers saw me and asked if I wanted some water. I said "Yes" and drank it. I went to the teller, cashed my check, and left! I did survive the anxiety attack, but it was em-barrassing! One other time I actually did faint when standing in line at McDonalds. Someone telephoned my brother to come and get me.

Anxiety can lead to other problems as well. For example, in 2018 a physician diagnosed me with aerophagia, which is a Latin word for swallowing air. Swallowing too much air has caused me to burp uncontrollably. Aerophagia can be caused by anxiety because when you feel anxious you swallow more air either from hyperventilating while talking or eating too fast. In the book, *The Bloated Belly Whisper* by Tamara Duker Freuman, she talks about aerophagia. She suggests treating this condition by taking anti-anxiety medica-tion or a muscle-relaxing medication. She also suggests seeing a cognitive behavioral therapist to learn breathing techniques.

Anxiety can be crippling but there are ways to deal with it. For me, first, getting enough sleep is critical. Second, taking anti-anxiety medication is helpful. I have taken Ativan, but it can be addictive, so I have to be careful about how much I take. There is a very helpful, free, support group called Recovery International that helps people deal with their anxiety. You can get information about this organization at *RecoveryInternational.org*.

Lastly, I would like to mention meditation. I am not very good at it, but if you study books and information at various websites you can get helpful tips on how to do it. It requires practice, but I believe it does calm you down. Also there is a new therapy called "floating." It involves simply floating in a pool of water to relax.

Schizophrenia And Smoking

During my lifetime I have been in contact with numerous people who have struggled with the disturbing symptoms associated with schizophrenia. Like many other people with some form of mental illness, a large number of people with schizophrenia have become addicted to nicotine and smoke cigarettes on a regular basis. From what I have read, I would say that people with schizophrenia or some other form of mental illness are far more likely to smoke than people in the general population.

On page 273 of his book, *Surviving Schizophrenia: A Manual for Families, Patients, and Providers*, (5th Edition), E. Fuller Torrey, M.D. stated that "Nicotine reduces anxiety, reduces sedation, and improves concentration in some people, which might be a form of self-medication for the person with schizophrenia." Because people with schizophrenia and other types of mental problems experience very stressful symptoms such as auditory or visual hallucinations, the habit of smoking may be perceived as helping relieve stress induced by these and other disturbing symptoms, however smoking contributes to a vast array of health problems.

For people who have become addicted to smoking, whether or not they are suffering from some form of mental illness, I recommend the book *How I Quit Smoking in 31 Days After Smoking for 32 Years*. In this book the author, Michael T. Petro, Jr., describes in detail how he quit smoking and says anyone can do so by following his simple but effective plan. I'm glad I never tried smoking!

Violence And Schizophrenia

In 2006 I had a terrifying experience. I have been a member of NAMI (National Alliance on Mental Illness) for years, and I have associated with other members of this helpful organization. Two of my associates were a guy named Albert and a girl named Lisa. I frequently told Albert that I thought Lisa's medication wasn't working, or that she wasn't taking her medication.

On March 23, 2006, when a NAMI meeting was over, I went outside to talk to other members. Lisa came up to me and asked, "Are we going to the bar tonight?" I told her, "No, we are going to the bookstore." Lisa became very angry and said, "Why do you like books, bitch?" I said, "I don't know." She then pushed me and tried to grab me. Terrified, I ran toward Nicole, the group leader, who was sitting in her car. I yelled, "Let me in!" Nicole let me in and locked the car door. Lisa came up to the car door, pounded on the window, and said, "I am going to kill you...you bitch."

Nicole started to drive off with me in her car, but Lisa got into her own car and pulled right next to Nicole's car. She gave us the finger, and then drove off. I reported this to the police, who said they would call her mental health agency and have her evaluated. One of the other NAMI members told me that Lisa was hearing voices that night. As discussed in the previous section titled "Understanding Voices," hearing voices is a classic symptom of schizophrenia. Albert had tried to tell Lisa's case worker and parents a long time ago that she wasn't behaving appropriately, but no one listened.

With schizophrenia, people could become violent if they don't receive the proper help, and schizophrenia is the most severe of all the mental illnesses because those who have it are not in touch with reality. When those with schizophrenia find a medication that works for them, they become stabilized. Once stabilized on medication, they can look back and remember some of the crazy thoughts they had and some of the crazy things they did. With or without medication, memory is retained, but with medication individuals with schizophrenia can look back and gain insight into how they behave when they are not taking their medication.

Suicide And Schizophrenia

According to the NAMI (National Alliance on Mental Illness) Greater Cleveland website, 90 percent of the people who die through suicide have been diagnosed with some form of mental illness.

People diagnosed with schizophrenia must take prescription medication. Without medication, suicide is seen as an option far too often. Sometimes, though, even people on medication commit suicide. For example, when I was in Dr. Herbert Meltzer's Clozapine (Clozaril) study, I became friends with a girl named Julie who also had schizophrenia. I don't know if she was taking her medication or not. I do know she would throw parties when her parents weren't home, and she would smoke pot and drink beer. I never joined the party people when they did that stuff. Shortly after one party, I had a routine session with my psychiatrist. "Have you seen Julie?" he asked me. I said "No," and he responded by saying that Julie shot herself in the head with a gun. I was shocked and devastated. I felt so sorry for her family.

I also had a brush with suicide before I was diagnosed with schizophrenia. From age 17 to age 20, I was depressed. I was so miserable I wanted to kill myself. I did go as far as to call the National Suicide Prevention Lifeline. Their telephone number is 1-800-273-8255. I don't remember the details of what we discussed, but I do remember that the call helped. According to the *Journal of the American Medical Association (JAMA)*, the medication Clozapine (Clozaril) reduces the risk of suicide. There is always help for any problem. Today, medications are far more effective in alleviating depression and suicidal thoughts than what we had in the past. If you are having suicidal thoughts, then it is time to get help. Do not isolate yourself. Suicidal thoughts are not accurate reflections of reality. Most importantly, keep in mind that suicide is a permanent solution to a temporary problem. It is a permanent solution to a temporary state of mind; therefore, it is the wrong solution. The website of the American Foundation for Suicide Prevention may be helpful.

My Mom's Advice To Other Parents

My mom says that the best advice she can give other parents is that you have to be patient. It takes time to find the right medication, and once found, it takes time for the medication to work. She told me some of the medications I was taking didn't work. Some worsened my condition and she would get frustrated with the doctors. She also says that being the parent of someone who has schizophrenia can be scary. For example, if the medication is not working right and you don't get help for that family member, it is possible they can harm you or themselves. No one else knows what their thoughts are, or what the voices are telling them to do.

Based on her observation of my behavior over a period of many years, she says the number one thing you shouldn't do is force a family member with schizophrenia to do things if you want him or her to get better. Most often, persuasion produces far better results than force. She also says people with schizophrenia need a lot of rest, so let them get enough sleep and don't label them as lazy or unmotivated!

Schizophrenia And Street Drugs

From what I have read, street drugs can produce symptoms similar to schizophrenia. So, before a doctor can diagnose someone with schizophrenia, he or she needs to do a drug test first to make sure street drugs are not causing the symptoms. Dual diagnosis is the condition of having a drug or alcohol problem as well as a mental illness.

Schizophrenia And Alzheimer's: The Similarities

One of the best ways I can describe schizophrenia is to compare some of it's symptoms with the symptoms of Alzheimer's. People with Alzheimer's and people with schizophrenia can experience hallucinations and delusions, and have no insight that they have a problem. My mom is a home health aide and her Alzheimer's client said one time to her, "Look at all the little children," but there were no children present. Similarly, when I was hospitalized, I remember thinking a lady and man on the psychiatric ward were friends of my mother, but they were not her friends – it was a delusion! Also, people with Alzheimer's and people with schizophrenia have difficulty organizing their thoughts, and a decreased ability to express emotions. They also tend to suffer short-term memory loss and sometimes they say things that do not make sense. Therefore, the symptoms of both illnesses tend to be similar.

Doctors

People suffering from mental illness often find it necessary to change doctors. I have seen several psychiatrists since I was diagnosed with schizophrenia. Some of these doctors were not very impressive. For example, one doctor ate lunch while talking to me. Another wanted to change my medication although she knew the medication I was taking was working well for me. (When a person is stabilized with a specific medication a good doctor would not want you to try other medications because it might involve being hospi-talized again.) Two doctors I saw while looking for a new psychia-trist (and was stabilized on medication) told me I needed to be rediagnosed without even knowing what I went through to get stabilized.

Remember the question, "What is a schizophrenic supposed to look like?" Did I not look schizophrenic to the doctors? They didn't even look at my records! I have found there are a lot of psychiatrists who do not specialize in schizophrenia. It's important to find a psychiatrist who does. I also recommend finding a psychiatrist who works out of a hospital in case you need to be hospitalized.

Also, it should be noted that a psychiatrist is a physician and therefore can prescribe medication; however, a psychologist is not a physician and consequently is limited to nonmedical psychotherapy. This is important because therapists cannot talk schizophrenics out of their biochemically-based symptoms; only medication can control such symptoms. A psychologist's talk therapy can be effective, but only after the individual has been stabilized on medication.

A psychiatrist I was seeing for five years died suddenly. This was certainly a devastating shock for his family and friends, but it was also very unfortunate for me, and perhaps for all his patients. He was always willing to see me when I had a problem; he made sure I was doing well on my medication, and he never tried to change my medication because he knew it was working well for me. He also listened to my problems and prescribed extra medication when I had terrible anxiety attacks. He served as an example of how a truly good psychiatrist should behave toward his or her patients.

Forensic Psychiatry

What is a forensic psychiatrist? What is a forensic patient? A forensic psychiatrist is a medical doctor who is trained in both law and mental health, and works with people who have psychiatric problems, such as schizophrenia. Forensic patients are those who have been accused of a crime and found unsuitable to stand trial because of a mental illness. Forensic patients are also those people who have been tried and found not guilty due to mental illness.

Medication

There are many medications for schizophrenia. Due to variations in body chemistry, medication that may work for one person may not work for another. Also, the time it takes for a given medication to work varies from one person to another. Antipsychotic medications such as Clozapine (Clozaril) are for people with serious mental health problems, such as schizophrenia. They work by affecting dopamine in the brain. The newer antipsychotics are called atypical, while the older antipsychotics are called conventional. Unlike many other medications, antipsychotics are not addictive.

I have tried conventional medications such as Haloperidol (Haldol), Loxapine (Loxitane), and many others. As stated earlier, I am now on the atypical antipsychotic medication Clozapine (Clozaril), which is used to treat severe schizophrenia symptoms in people who have not responded well to other medications. Patients who take Clozapine (Clozaril) will have their blood levels tested every two weeks for the first six months of treatment. After that, it can be tested on a monthly basis.

When I first started taking Clozapine (Clozaril) for Dr. Herbert Meltzer's study, I was put on 200 mg doses. With that dosage I needed only five to six hours of sleep each night. When the study was over, they took me off Clozapine (Clozaril) and tried other medications that didn't work, so they put me back on Clozapine (Clozaril) and increased my dosage to 350 mg. With this dosage I now need 12 hours of sleep. The higher the dose, the more sedation!

I take my medication every night at 11:30 p.m. and wake up around 11:30 a.m. I am not a morning person, and most people with schizophrenia are not due to medication sedation. I have tried to take my medication earlier to get up earlier and it never works. I always wake up in the late morning no matter how early I take my medication.

One thing that disrupts my sleep is drinking caffeinated liquids before bedtime. I can toss and turn for hours. Here are some helpful sleep tips: Try a glass of warm, unsweetened almond milk. Keep your room completely dark. Make sure you're not too cold or too hot. Don't sleep with your TV or phone on. Don't think about problems at night. Try to go to bed at the same time every night. If I go to bed really late and take my medication really late, I could spend the whole next day in bed. Sometimes reading will help you fall asleep. Try not to take naps, otherwise you may toss and turn at night. Wear socks to bed to keep your feet warm which helps you to relax.

Oftentimes people do not take medication because they fear side effects. I have been on many medications with side effects. For example, one medication gave me weird movements, one made me lie in bed all day, and one gave me blurred vision. The only side effects for the one I am on now are drooling at night, heavy sedation, and weight gain. But with schizophrenia you must take medication because that is the only thing that can control your intrusive thoughts. Nothing else will work! The side effects I experience from the medication are nothing compared to the symptoms of schizophrenia, such as paranoia.

Some medications can cause tardive dyskinesia when used long-term. This is a condition similar to Tourette syndrome wherein the patient experiences uncontrolled muscle movements. When taking the medication Haldol one of my arms would move up and down involuntarily. I have a friend who fumbles his fingers involuntarily as a result of treatment with antipsychotic medication. This movement disorder may develop months, years, or perhaps many decades after taking certain antipsychotic medications.

Unfortunately, there is no known cure for tardive dyskinesia. That's why it's important to identify the symptoms as soon as possible. Lowering the dose or switching to another medication may be necessary when symptoms are observed. Fortunately for me and many other people with schizophrenia, tardive dyskinesia is not known to be a side effect of Clozapine (Clozaril).

For those who do not have insurance to pay for medication, there are patient assistance programs that can be very helpful. For example, some patients who meet certain eligibility requirements set by pharmaceutical companies may actually receive free prescription medication. It is very important to have a good relationship with your pharmacist as well. A good pharmacist can answer questions about side effects, medication interactions, and can tell you exactly how to take your medication and what to do if you miss a dose or take it incorrectly. I am very pleased with the pharmacy I go to and wouldn't go anywhere else.

Starting on February 28, 2019, in order to get Clozapine (Clozaril) pharmacies and physicians must enroll in the Clozapine REMS (Risk Evaluation Mitigation Strategy) program. The FDA (Federal Drug Administration) requires the certification because of the risk of severe neutropenia. The PDA (Pre-Dispense Authorization) is mandatory.

Denial

Sometimes mentally ill people are in denial that they have schizophrenia and they don't want to accept their diagnosis; sometimes family members are in denial and they might say things like, "Oh, just snap out of it!" With schizophrenia, you cannot just snap out of it. Also, no one causes it, it is a chemical imbalance in the brain.

It is common for those with schizophrenia to think they are not ill, and thus believe they have no need for antipsychotic medication. This is called anosognosia.

Some state laws say a person cannot be forced to take medication, but I feel that individuals with schizophrenia should be required to take medication because they could be a danger to themselves or others. Also, when people are initially discharged from a hospital, someone has to make sure they take their medication in order to prevent a relapse.

How To Avoid Relapse

First and foremost, accept the fact that you have an illness. Secondly, do not stop taking your medication because you feel better. You are feeling better precisely because you are taking your medication as prescribed by your doctor!

Lastly, keep in mind that poor grooming (See Grooming And Schizophrenia) lack of motivation, self-isolation, and poor sleeping are all signs of relapse!

Nutrition And Health

Nutrition is extremely important for people who have schizophrenia because we are on medication for life. By eating right we can enjoy a healthy life. Unfortunately, the medication Clozapine (Clozaril) can cause agranulocytosis, which, as stated earlier, is a low white blood cell count. Currently, I am following the Blood Type A food, beverage, and supplement lists from *Eat Right for Your Type* by Peter J. D'Adamo, M.D. (Berkeley Books, 2002). On page five of this book Dr. D'Adamo says, "When you eat the foods for your blood type the highly beneficial foods act as a medicine, the neutral foods act like a food, and the avoid foods act like a poison in your body." If it were not for the Blood Type diet, my white blood cell counts would be really low.

According to medical science, there are four different blood types, which include 0, A, B, and AB. For more information regarding the types of diets recommended for the four different blood types, the reader is encouraged to go to the website, *4YourType.com*, and check out the information provided.

25

My blood type is A+, and these are some of the things that I swear raise my white blood cell count: molasses on plain yogurt, aloe vera drinks, carrot juice, and decaffeinated green tea. I consume absolutely no artificial sweeteners and no alcohol; they always lower my white blood cell count. Your body pH is another factor to consider in maintaining good overall health. You can monitor your pH, or the degree to which your body is acidic or alkaline, by testing your urine with pH strips that can be purchased online. At the website *DrDavidWilliams.com*, it is stated that, to prevent disease, the human body should be slightly alkaline. To make your body more alkaline, go online and Google "alkaline foods" and choose the correct foods for your blood type.

Here are some health tips I have learned:

1. A good carbohydrate will have the word "whole" on the food label. If it does not say "whole," it is not a healthy carb.

2. Sodium should not be higher than calories.

3. I never buy anything with high fructose corn syrup. It can be in breads, cereals, yogurts, and beverages, so read labels.

4. I never buy anything with hydrogenated oils. They clog arteries and so do foods with lots of oil in them. Read labels.

5. Foods that raise cholesterol are roasted nuts (look for raw instead) and cheese. When I overeat cheese, I gain weight quickly because it is a high-fat food.

6. If you are going to eat hot dogs or lunch meat, look on the label for meats without nitrates.

7. If you eat bread, sprouted breads are healthier. Try Ezekiel bread!

I have read that omega 3's are healthy for the brain. I get my omega 3's through my diet. Some things I eat are: salmon, walnuts, foods with flax seeds, chia seeds, and eggs with omega 3's. Also from what I have read, some books say gluten in foods can cause schizophrenia. As a child I had an allergy to wheat (which contains gluten). I also found out that I have an intolerance to gluten. Some books have also said that schizophrenia symptoms can be reduced by eating gluten-free. But remember, eating gluten-free will not cure schizophrenia – you still need medication!

In March 2015, I went to a holistic nutritionist. By looking at my eyes she could tell I had Candida, also called Candida albicans. Candida is a yeast that grows naturally in the intestines. Prescription medications can destroy the friendly bacteria in your intestines, causing an overgrowth of Candida yeast.

Candida yeast overgrowth may also be caused by too much sugar in the diet. The Candida diet is a sugar-free diet and I do not mean eating sugar-free sweeteners. I mean eliminating sugar and all other sweeteners from your diet! The holistic nutritionist told me to add coconut oil to my diet because it contains caprylic acid, which helps to reduce Candida yeast.

Almost every person I know on medication for a mental illness has a bloated stomach, which I believe is caused by prescription medication. Remember, Candida is a yeast overgrowth problem. If you make bread and add yeast, the bread rises! I believe the yeast growth caused by prescription medication can bloat the stomach.

So, to combat this side effect I take probiotic supplements and eat foods containing probiotics such as yogurt, kefir, and sour cream!

Perhaps, most importantly, probiotics have never reduced my white blood cell counts; instead, they have actually made them go up. I also believe probiotics have helped prevent me from getting the stomach flu.

According to many reputable websites (including that of the U.S. Food and Drug Administration), some prescription medications may have a toxic effect on the liver. So to cleanse my liver, I squeeze a little lemon juice in a glass of water before drinking it. In addition to detoxifying the liver, this simple formula can also be used to improve digestion.

For those living in the Northeastern Ohio area who are searching for someone to guide them through natural forms of therapy, I recommend Dr. Jane Semple, M.A., N.D. This naturopathic doctor operates the Alternative Healing Institute located at 4965 Dover Center Road in North Olmstead, Ohio. Her telephone number is 440-777-2665. She has been very helpful in guiding me through the choices I have made regarding natural approaches to health care.

Many people with schizophrenia live on a restricted income, and not by choice. Buying a sufficient amount of healthy food can be a struggle. To buy healthy foods less expensively, keep in mind that Whole Foods has their own organic brand called 365 with great prices. Giant Eagle also has their own organic brand called Nature's Basket. Trader Joe's and Wal-Mart are loaded with inexpensive organic foods. If you are looking for inexpensive gluten-free foods, try Aldi's and Big Lots.

Supplements

I am not a physician, so I am not offering medical advice here or anywhere else in this book; instead, I am simply providing the reader with what I have learned over the years regarding supplements and medication interactions. If you are taking any type of medication always consult with your doctor before taking any supplements. This is vital because some supplements may interact with your medication and cause undesirable side effects. Also, keep in mind that what works for me may not work for you because my body chemistry may be very different from yours.

I take a multivitamin and Vitamin D3. My doctor said my body chemistry was low in Vitamin D3, so I take 1,000 IU each day. I have found that taking Vitamin D3 helps reduce my anxiety level and also eases depression.

Recipes

I have assembled a variety of recipes. I have found that each of the recipes below produces foods that are both nutritious and delicious. I hope you enjoy them as much as I do.

Tofu Chocolate Mousse

- 12 oz. soft tofu, drained
- ¼ cup cacao powder
- ⅓ cup maple syrup
- 1 tablespoon instant coffee granules

Process tofu, cacao powder, maple syrup, and coffee granules in a food processor or blender until smooth. Eat right away, or refrigerate overnight. It tastes like pudding.

Tofu with Almond Butter Sauce

- 1 package of extra firm tofu
- ¼ cup almond butter
- ¼ cup water
- 1-2 tablespoons honey

Slice and warm the tofu. Next, to make the almond butter sauce, stir other ingredients together and warm them and then pour almond butter sauce over tofu. Enjoy!

Zucchini Soup

- 1 carton of vegetable broth
- 4-5 zucchini, sliced with the skin intact

Bring broth to a boil. Add zucchini and boil until the zucchini is soft. Cool. Blend in blender until it looks like soup. Reheat and enjoy!

Tofu Chili

- 1 package of pumpkin soup
- 3 cans of beans, any kind, drained
- 1 cup of chopped celery
- Package extra firm tofu (16 oz.), cut into bite-size pieces
- Sour cream (optional)

Combine pumpkin soup, beans, celery, and tofu. Bring to a boil. When heated add sour cream if desired, and enjoy!

Mashed Cauliflower

- 1 bag frozen cauliflower
- 3 tablespoons butter
- ¼ cup of milk

Add cauliflower to boiling water and boil until soft. Drain, then add milk and butter. Mash and enjoy!

Avocado Smoothie

- ½ avocado
- 1 cup unsweetened almond milk
- 1 teaspoon raw honey
- 2 teaspoons chia seeds
- 1 teaspoon cinnamon

Blend. Makes one serving. Enjoy!

Deviled Avocado Eggs

- 1 whole avocado
- 12 eggs
- Mayonnaise (as much as you want)

Hard boil eggs. Cool and cut eggs in half; take out yolks, set them aside. Mix avocado with egg yolks and mayonnaise. Put mixture into egg whites. Enjoy!

Hot Chocolate (Serves 2)

- 2 cups milk
- ¼ cup cacao powder
- 1 teaspoon molasses
- 1 teaspoon ground cinnamon
- ½ teaspoon vanilla extract

Add all ingredients in a small saucepan. Whisk over medium heat until cacao powder is incorporated and mixture is hot, about five minutes. Be sure not to let the milk scald.

Fitness And Medication

Before I was diagnosed with schizophrenia, I was always thin and could never gain weight. In 10th grade, I weighed 95 pounds. I would eat a lot of food but would never gain weight. However, when I was taking the medication Haldol, I went from 115 to 180 pounds. I believe the weight gain occurred because while taking Haldol, I would lie in bed all day and only get up to eat. When I was switched to Clozapine (Clozaril), I no longer spent the day in bed. But even on Clozapine (Clozaril) I have gained weight, and feel my medication increases my appetite. So, I walk to stay slim. I try to walk two miles five days per week. I also joined a free group called Food Addicts Anonymous, a group that deals with people who tend to overeat. Google "Food Addicts Anonymous" to find a group in your area.

Grooming And Schizophrenia

While many women and men with schizophrenia are well-groomed, many others are not. There was a time I wouldn't shower because I thought people could see me while I was in the shower. Also, I know one woman's son who has schizophrenia who did not shower for a month and I suggested she get him to the hospital as soon as possible. Therefore, not showering or not bathing could be a sign of schizophrenia, or relapse.

Where To Go For Psychiatric Help In The Cleveland, Ohio Area!

Saint Vincent Charity Hospital And Medical Center

Although I have never been a patient at Saint Vincent Charity Hospital and Medical Center, through my research I have concluded that it may offer the very best psychiatric care in the Cleveland, Ohio area. Their Psychiatric Emergency Department is operational 24/7, and it is one of only two hospitals in Ohio that offers such around-the-clock psychiatric emergency care. This facility is known throughout the region for its expertise in behavioral health, and is staffed with psychiatrists, psychiatric nurses, social workers, and mental health technicians. Inpatient services include the following: comprehensive assessment, crisis intervention, occupational therapy, recreational therapy, chemical dependency treatment, medication management, psycho-educational groups and individual interactions, and patient and family education. Psychiatric care as well as alcohol and other drug dependency care are also provided through outpatient services. Lastly, Saint Vincent Charity Hospital and Medical Center offers geropsychiatric services for older adults experiencing memory loss, dementia, and other mental health problems.

University Hospitals
Connor Integrative Health Network

Those with mental health problems may wish to explore a specialty called "integrative psychiatry," offered by University Hospitals of Cleveland, Ohio. At their website, the visitor discovers that the University Hospitals Connor Integrative Health Network "offers integrative psychiatry to enable patients to get in touch with and engage the body's natural healing abilities. This holistic mind-body therapy is designed to enhance the whole person and it benefits patients with [a variety of] conditions." Anxiety, chronic pain, depression, insomnia, fatigue, and stress-related problems are listed as conditions that may be addressed with integrative psychiatry.

At their website it is noted that integrative psychiatry "moves beyond medications," and is offered as a "holistic therapy." This form of therapy is based on the logical notion that one's mental health is impacted by many interconnected factors such as one's biology, environment, beliefs, family dynamics, and constitution. Yoga, guided imagery, talk therapy, and massage and meditation are among the "mind-body treatments" that "move beyond medication and diagnoses, and emphasize the healing power within."

As one who has experienced a variety of treatments over the years, I am intrigued by the natural approach outlined for integrative psychiatry. However, while treatments other than medication may be beneficial, based on my personal experience I believe that medication is central to any treatment plan designed for people struggling with schizophrenia.

The web address that will take you directly to the webpage containing the above information and numerous informative links is as follows:

http://www.uhConnorIntegrativeHealth.org/services/integrative-psychiatry.

To schedule an integrative psychiatry appointment one is directed to call 216-285-4070.

Additional Support Services

Magnolia Clubhouse In Cleveland, Ohio

When I first got out of the hospital in 1990, I went to a place called Hill House. Today, it is called Magnolia Clubhouse. Just recently, in 2015, I decided to go to Magnolia Clubhouse with a friend from the NAMI group to check it out. I discovered they provide lunch from 12:00 p.m. to 1:00 p.m. For one dollar per day they have self-improvement activities, and can help you find employment and doctor services. Also I discovered at Magnolia Clubhouse, they have a nutrition group, yoga, Zumba, meditation, and fun activities. To become a member you must have a mental illness. I rave about this place especially for people who just got out of the hospital.

NAMI Greater Cleveland

NAMI, the National Alliance on Mental Illness, is a great resource for people with mental health challenges. Group meetings are available for people with mental illness, as well as for their family members and other caregivers. The general public is also welcome to attend community education meetings hosted by mental health professionals. For only $5.00 one can become a member of NAMI and receive newsletters such as *NAMI Voice* and *News Briefs,* and the magazine titled, *Advocate.* Google "NAMI" to locate numerous informative websites.

Volunteering On The Psychiatric Ward

The most rewarding thing I do is volunteering on the psychiatric ward at a local hospital, where I promote NAMI Greater Cleveland. The patients really appreciate me. Here are some of the things I have learned from volunteering:

Some of these patients have never heard of NAMI.

They usually do not want to admit they have a mental illness.

They usually believe they do not need medication.

Some patients are very ill. They look normal on the outside, but when they speak, you can tell they are very ill. For example, one man with schizophrenia said to me, "I know how I got schizophrenia — a roach was on my birthday cake!" And there was a woman who said, "Someone transplanted my brain."

Some patients stay in the hospital for a while, and some come and go more quickly. Today, hospitals don't keep patients as long as they used to, probably due to their insurance requirements rather than the mental health needs of the patient. Because of this, it is possible that people will leave the hospital before they are properly stabilized.

Group Homes

Not all mentally ill people can take good care of themselves. Some need to live in a group home. A group home is a place where people who need supervised care or attention live together in a group. I have a friend who went to my old clinic. Her father put her in a group home after her mother died. She hates it. She says she has no freedom, strict rules, and has to wake up early for her medication and breakfast. She also told me that the group home owner is mean. Almost every time my mom and I call to take her out, the group home owner will not let her go. We don't understand why!

I have another friend who lives in a group home, and this is what he told me: "You can have a roommate or a private room. Some residents are high-functioning (meaning they can drive) and some are low-functioning. Sometimes the food is horrible." This concerns me because people on medication need to eat healthy foods. He also said, "Someone does the cleaning and laundry for you. No activities! There is a curfew of 9:00 p.m. Sometimes they will call the police if you leave without signing out. Most residents go to bed at 9:00 p.m. and wake up at 7:00 a.m. to take medication, but you can go back to bed. Medications are delivered to the group home. You have to take the bus or drive to your doctor's appointments."

My mother told me that before they released me from the hospital, they told her she should consider putting me in a group home. She said the only way she would consider it was if she could visit a group home herself to see what it was like. When she visited one, she thought that the people there were walking around like zombies, and she would never consider putting me there. My mom is not even sure who checks these group homes to see how well they take care of the residents.

Movies About Schizophrenia
You Should Consider Watching

Canvas: This movie is a true story of a mother who struggled with schizophrenia. I loved this movie! It really shows how people with schizophrenia can act when not taking medication or realizing they have a problem. At *HealthCentral.com*, I found the following movie critique: "It is a rare event when a motion picture presents paranoid schizophrenia in a responsible and accurate light...The movie is a remarkably honest and unembellished account of a father and a ten-year-old son's firsthand experiences with a mother attempting to cope with schizophrenia, a mother who loves both of them dearly despite her illness." Robin Cunningham, who wrote the critique of *Canvas*, said this movie was "exceptionally well done." He further stated that it could "play an important role in fighting mental health stigma."

A Beautiful Mind: A Beautiful Mind is based on a true story. It covers the life of John Nash, who suffered from the classical symptoms of schizophrenia. Nash was a mathematical genius who taught at Princeton University. In spite of his mental illness, in 1994 he won the Nobel Memorial Prize in Economic Sciences. He also received the Abel Prize, which is considered to be one of the most prestigious honors one can receive in the field of mathematics. John Nash was a gifted mathematician who excelled despite his schizophrenia.

A friend from my high school once told me that I said there was fire coming out of my drawers. Of course, there really was no fire there. People struggling with schizophrenia see things that aren't really there, and this movie provides excellent examples of how they experience visual and auditory hallucinations. The movie demonstrates in a very instructional way how they have great difficulty distinguishing imaginary characters from real people.

The Soloist: This movie is about a black man, Nathaniel Anthony Ayers, who was a Julliard College dropout. (Once when I went to Magnolia Clubhouse, one of the workers there told me that Nathaniel used to play his cello right on a corner near Magnolia Avenue!) Nathaniel dropped out of school and became homeless as a result of his struggle with schizophrenia. The movie shows how this gifted musician survived on the mean streets of Los Angeles. That is where Nathaniel meets Steve Lopez, a *Los Angeles Times* columnist. Steve tries to help Nathaniel by getting him an apartment through a mental health agency called LAMP.

I liked this movie, but I didn't agree with one comment made by the guy who played the part of the LAMP employee. He said, "Nathaniel doesn't need one more person telling him he needs medication." I disagree. I think any mental health agency should promote medication, because people with schizophrenia cannot recognize that they have a problem. In this movie, Nathaniel didn't think he needed medication. I hope to this day that Nathaniel is doing well. Everyone with schizophrenia should be encouraged to find the proper medication through his or her doctor.

Love & Mercy: In 2015 the movie *Love & Mercy* was released. This is a very informative movie about the life of Brian Wilson, a songwriter and cofounder of the Beach Boys. Unknown to many Americans, this gifted individual was diagnosed with paranoid schizophrenia, and he faced all the challenges that others have had to endure when given this potentially debilitating diagnosis. But despite his illness, he overcame very difficult hardships and helped make the Beach Boys an extremely popular and successful musical group.

The story of the life of Brian Wilson — as told in *Love & Mercy* — serves as an inspiration to all who are faced with any sort of serious challenge. Whether you are forced to deal with psychological problems, financial problems, marital problems, physical problems, or whatever, this movie can inspire the viewer with the courage needed to face and overcome any and all of life's challenges.

Not only did Brian Wilson have to battle the voices in his head, he also had to deal with the misguided voice and counter-productive behavior of his therapist. His over-controlling therapist, as depicted in this movie, may have done more harm than good in his interactions with his patient, Brian Wilson. What everyone can learn from this film is that choice of a therapist is critical, and must not be taken lightly. Try to find a therapist you like, who shows you compassion, and whose therapeutic style works for you.

Love & Mercy is an outstanding movie, and should be viewed by all mental health professionals, students, patients, and their family members! I watched it, enjoyed it, learned from it, and was inspired by it! I hope it will do the same for you!

Reading Material About Schizophrenia You Should Consider Reviewing

I recommend three books: *To Cry a Dry Tear*, by Bill McPhee; *The Quiet Room*, by Lori Schiller; and *Surviving Schizophrenia*, by E. Fuller Torrey, M.D. I also recommend an article in the February, 2016 issue of *Reader's Digest* titled, *What It's Like To Be A Person With Schizophrenia*.

Dr. Lillian Glass, a psychologist, is reportedly a "body language expert," and has appeared on many television shows to analyze the body language of others, especially celebrities. Dr. Glass has appeared on programs such as *Dr. Phil, Nicole Grace, The Insider, Entertainment Tonight,* and other popular television programs. She has also authored many books, such as *The Body Language of Liars*, *Toxic Men, Toxic People*, and many others.

In reading Dr. Glass's book, *Toxic People*, I found that I was disappointed by the manner in which she describes what she refers to as the "mental case." You may wish to read this book to see if you agree with me.

The most helpful website about schizophrenia I have ever seen is SARDAA.org. (SARDAA stands for Schizophrenia and Related Disorders Alliance of America.) At this website there are blogs, videos, and newsletters with the latest information on schizophrenia. Another helpful website is called *BringChangeToMind.org*.

Dating And Schizophrenia

Although I have never checked out these websites myself, there are two websites for people with a mental illness who would like to try dating. The two sites are as follows: *TrueAcceptance.com* and *NoLongerLonely.com*.

People May Use Your Illness Against You

I tried to break up in a nice way with one boyfriend, but he continued to show up at places I visited, and he would also e-mail me. I started to get angry about it, so I sent him an e-mail saying I was planning to get a restraining order if he didn't leave me alone. He e-mailed me back that he had already told the police about my condition. After reading that e-mail, I cried. He tried to make me look unstable by bringing my mental illness into the situation, when all I wanted to do was break up with him.

His father, who is an optometrist and not a psychiatrist, would constantly tell me that I didn't have schizophrenia. Again, what is a schizophrenic supposed to look like?

Stigma And Discrimination

I had severe ear popping and went to several ear doctors. None of them could figure out the cause of this problem. One of the doctors said the ear popping was normal, though severe ear popping to me is not normal. I eventually saw a TMJ (temporo-mandibular joint disorder) specialist, whom my dentist recommended. He said it was TMJ and sold me mouth splints, which did nothing.

When I went to an ear doctor at a local hospital, I was asked what medications I was taking. I said I was taking Clozapine (Clozaril) for schizophrenia, and I feel they discriminated against me based upon my response. I got copies of my medical records from the ear doctors to read what they said about me, and they kept mentioning "paranoid schizophrenia." One of the ear doctors said to my face, "I don't mean to call you crazy, but this problem is in your head!" He also asked me right out, "What is your diagnosis?" (He already knew my diagnosis because he put it in my records.) I answered him by asking, "What does my diagnosis have to do with my ear problem?" He answered, "Everything."

This worried me because these doctors were talking more about my diagnosis than they were about my ear problem. He conducted a pressure test and found excessive pressure in both ears. He said he could insert tubes in my ears to relieve the excessive pressure, but I was so humiliated by what he said that I would not allow him to do so. I cried when I left the doctor's office. I silently asked myself, "Who cries when leaving a doctor's office after seeking help?" Later, I allowed another ear doctor to put tubes in my ears to relieve the excessive pressure. This was the only treatment that improved my ear popping problem.

I have a psychiatrist who I see once a month. So, why would I go to an ear doctor for a psychiatric problem, or vice versa? This upset me so much that I went to the hospital's ombudsman office. Basically that did nothing but make me upset once again. The ombudsman sent me a letter in the mail in response to my concerns.

In the letter the ombudsman noted that I had "expressed concerns" about an unpleasant interaction with one of their physicians. She acknowledged that my main concern was that Dr. X (of course, that's not his real name) seemed to concentrate more on my mental illness than on my ear problem.

The ombudsman said that she shared my concerns with Dr. X directly, and Dr. X "apologizes for your concern." The ombudsman said Dr. X wanted to explain how my mental illness may "play a role in other medical conditions." My concern about Dr. X had been recorded, and sorrow was expressed about my dissatisfaction with the services I had received. The letter ended with a "Thank you" from the ombudsman, and it was further stated that they "continuously strive to improve" their services and are "grateful" I shared my experience with them.

The ombudsman office is supposed to help you if you have a problem with a medical service, if you have questions about the care you received, if you have concerns about any employees, if the health care facility did not provide satisfactory service during inpatient or outpatient care, or if you have a billing complaint related to your medical care.

Based on my experiences in dealing with doctors and others, I learned that just about anyone can discriminate against a person who has received the diagnosis of schizophrenia. No matter who he or she may be dealing with, if there is a conflict or a misunderstanding, the person with schizophrenia will always be viewed as "the wrong one," and will therefore be seen as the source of the problem. So, it is much more difficult for people who have schizophrenia to defend their point of view or their rights because they are assumed to be the cause of any conflict or misunderstanding. While this can be very frustrating, it is worsened by the fact that I have known so-called "normal" people who don't act as normal as me when I am on my medication and quite stable. However, these "normal" people are still less likely than a person with schizophrenia to be the victim of discrimination.

Schizophrenia And The Workplace

The Americans with Disabilities Act (ADA) protects disabled people's rights in the workplace. If you have been discriminated against while trying to get a job or while on the job, you need to contact a civil rights attorney.

Schizophrenia: Let's Call It Something Else!

Bill MacPhee, the publisher of *SZ Magazine* (formerly known as *Schizophrenia Digest*), launched a campaign in 2015 to change the name of schizophrenia in order to stop the stigma. He mentions in an online article that the image the public has of a person with schizophrenia is that of a potentially violent killer or a disheveled homeless person wandering the streets. He has suggested the mental health community adopt the term "MacPhee syndrome," supposedly to "put a face" on this form of illness. Because Bill MacPhee has been diagnosed with schizophrenia, but is a successful, high-functioning person who publishes *SZ Magazine*, he believes "MacPhee syndrome" would convey the message that people with this illness are not scary, dysfunctional people.

My mom and I agree that we do not like the term schizophrenia. Over the years, people have come to identify schizophrenia as a totally scary word. When people hear the words schizophrenia or schizophrenic, they automatically think these words mean the same thing as "crazy," "lunatic," "insane," or "psychopath." Did you know that schizophrenia used to be called "dementia praecox?" My mom had an old dictionary, *The Reader's Digest Great Encyclopedic Dictionary*, published by Funk and Wagnall in 1975. Here is its definition for schizophrenia: "Any group of psychotic disorders characterized by delusional formations, a retreat from reality, conflicting emotions, and deterioration of personality; formerly called dementia praecox." We feel neither label is accurate. We think it should be called "thought disorder," because that is precisely what is experienced by the individual. One's thoughts are confused and disordered. People with schizophrenia have difficulty distinguishing between what is real and what is imaginary, and that can be very confusing!

I hope this book will inspire mental health professionals to replace the term schizophrenia with a label that is descriptive but not frightening and not misunderstood by the general public. I think it would be a relief to all who have received the diagnosis of schizophrenia!

So, What Is A Schizophrenic Supposed To Look Like?

How do we answer the question, "What is a schizophrenic supposed to look like?" To put that question in perspective, we may ask the following questions: What does an obsessive-compulsive look like? What does a bipolar look like? What does a diabetic look like? What does a hemophiliac look like? We could also ask, what does a teacher look like? What does an author look like? What does an accountant look like? After all, a teacher, an author, or an accountant may or may not have schizophrenia!

To determine what a schizophrenic looks like we must say, it depends on the individual and it depends on the current circumstance in which we find that individual. A schizophrenic on medication may look very different from another schizophrenic not taking medication.

Certainly, a diabetic very low on insulin may look like a very different person when he or she has an adequate amount of insulin circulating through their bloodstream. Likewise, a well-rested healthy person may look like a different person when sleep-deprived! When describing a so-called "normal" person, don't we sometimes hear someone say, "He isn't himself today," or "She isn't herself today?"

Remember, one out of every one hundred people you meet has schizophrenia. Have you been able to identify which ones have schizophrenia? Have you been able to pick them out of a crowd at the mall, at the supermarket, or at a sporting event? An honest person must answer "No," to these questions. The answer to the question, what is a schizophrenic supposed to look like, can only be based on preconceived notions, many of which will be incorrect when applied to a specific individual at a particular point in time! Most importantly, it should be noted that outer appearance may often have nothing to do with an internal, biochemically-based illness that you cannot see. So, please don't look at a person stabilized on medication and say, "You do not look schizophrenic on the outside." People with schizophrenia look as normal as anyone else!

Special Notes From The Author

I want the reader to know that the names of some people discussed in this book have been changed to protect their privacy. Also, the names of some people have simply been omitted.

Please note that none of the information presented in this book is to be considered medical advice. Before making any changes to your medical treatment plan, your diet, or your intake of nutritional supplements, always consult with your physician or other health care professional.

I would also like to address the concern that some people have regarding the use of the term "schizophrenic." Although I use the words "schizophrenic" and "schizophrenia" throughout this book, the reader still finds the heading, "Schizophrenia: Let's Call It Something Else!" My mother and I agree that the word "schizophrenia" is scary to us and to many other people as well.

Those who object to the use of the term "schizophrenic" prefer to use words such as "a person with schizophrenia," or "a person who has schizophrenia." I agree that the terms "schizophrenia" and "schizophrenic" should be replaced with words that are less scary and less disturbing; however, both terms are commonly used today, so I wrote this book using words that most people would easily understand.

In addition, we must all recognize that there is a highly successful support group called Alcoholics Anonymous that is widely accepted by people who are grappling with alcoholism. Similarly, there is a support group called Schizophrenics Anonymous that is readily accepted by people who are struggling with schizophrenia, which can be located at the website *SARDAA.org.* Just recently they changed the name of this group from Schizophrenics Anonymous to Schizophrenia Alliance perhaps due to the stigma attached to the word schizophrenic, however, when this book was published both names were still in use.

Lastly, as indicated elsewhere in this book, I was admitted to the psychiatric ward of a hospital under an Emergency Certificate. Laws vary across the 50 states, but generally an individual can be forced by state law to enter or remain in a mental health facility against his or her will when an Emergency Certificate is signed by an authorized person. The authorized person is usually an attending psychiatrist, but other mental health workers may also be authorized in some states.

The initial detention is usually for a period of 72 hours. During this time the staff is authorized to observe the individual, conduct an assessment to arrive at a diagnosis, and prepare and implement a treatment plan. If the individual is determined to be a danger to himself, or a danger to others, or is considered to be gravely disabled, the involuntary detention can be extended.

For example, in Ohio a person can be detained involuntarily for 72 hours for observation, diagnosis, and treatment. If deemed necessary, emergency hospitalization may be extended for an additional 48 hours under a TOD or Temporary Order of Detention. During this time period a court will determine if further hospitalization is needed.

For information regarding involuntary detention in a mental health facility in your state, the reader is encouraged to conduct an Internet search. State governments and educational centers have made detailed information readily available to the general public.

About The Author

This work represents Lori Rochat's fourth edition of her first book titled, *What is a Schizophrenic Supposed to Look Like?* Having overcome many challenges in her life, she now invests her time, energy, knowledge, and experience performing volunteer work on a psychiatric ward where she shares her insight into schizophrenia with the patients.

Lori earned a NAMI (National Alliance on Mental Illness) Peer-to-Peer Education Program Certificate of Achievement to better serve others who have received the diagnosis of schizophrenia. In 2009 she attended free nutrition classes offered through the Ohio State University Extension program, and earned a Certificate in Expanded Food and Nutrition Education.

While constantly seeking to expand her knowledge of general health, nutrition, mental health, and other important topics, Lori volunteers for the NAMI Speakers Bureau and has given presentations to nurses in training at the Saint Vincent Charity Hospital and Medical Center in Cleveland, Ohio. She continues to seek new ways to educate the public and provide assistance to others who have received the diagnosis of schizophrenia.